Fat Bombs

Keto Fat Bombs

Ketogenic Diet Fat Bombs That You MUST Prepare Before Any Other!

Introduction

When most people hear the words "fat bomb" what comes to mind is unhealthy foods and undesirable weight gain. Well, this is not the case, especially when you are on the Ketogenic diet.

Why is that so, you may wonder?

Fat bombs are just food with 85% or more fat.

In fact, Ketogenic fat bombs can give you the much needed energy boost by supplying an instant dose of healthy fats paired with minimal proteins and very low amounts of carbs, which makes them perfect tools for getting into ketosis.

Lucky for you, this book will get straight to introducing you to over 50 mouth-watering keto fat bombs recipes that you MUST prepare!

By reading this book, you will realize that you don't even need to obsess about sugary desserts while on the keto diet, as you will have fat bombs that will keep you full without getting you out of ketosis.

Let's begin!

Your Free Gifts

As a way of thanking you for the purchase, I'd like to offer you 2 complimentary gifts:

- **How To Get Through Any Weight Loss Plateau While On The Ketogenic Diet:** The title is self-explanatory; if you are struggling with getting off a weight loss plateau while on the Keto diet, you will find this free gift very eye opening on what has been ailing you. <u>Grab your copy now by clicking/tapping here</u> or simply enter <u>http://bit.ly/2fantonpubketo</u> into your browser.

- **5 Pillar Life Transformation Checklist:** This short book is about life transformation, presented in bit size pieces for easy implementation. I believe that without such a checklist, you are likely to have a hard time implementing anything in this book and any other thing you set out to do religiously and sticking to it for the long haul. It doesn't matter whether your goals relate to weight loss, relationships, personal finance, investing, personal development, improving communication in your family, your overall health, finances, improving your sex life, resolving issues in your relationship, fighting PMS successfully, investing, running a successful business, traveling etc. With a checklist like this one, you can bet that anything you do will seem a lot easier to implement until the end. Therefore, even if you don't continue reading this book, at least read the one thing that will help you in every other aspect of your life. <u>Grab your copy now by clicking/tapping here</u> or simply enter <u>http://bit.ly/2fantonfreebie</u> into your browser. Your life will never be the same again (if you implement what's in this book), I promise.

PS: I'd like your feedback. If you are happy with this book, please leave a review on Amazon.

Table of Contents

PS:

I have special interest in the Ketogenic diet. My wife has been following the Ketogenic diet and I can honestly say that the journey has been amazing. The diet works. And this is why I have committed to writing and publishing as many of the Ketogenic diet books as possible to give readers different options as far as the Ketogenic diet is concerned.

For instance, I have Ketogenic diet books exclusively dedicated for:

- Breakfast

- Main Meals

- Snacks

- Desserts

- Appetizers

- Soups

- Vegetarians

- Crockpot/slow cooker users

- Instant pot users

- Air fryer users

- People who are on the Paleo diet

- People who are following intermittent fasting

- People who are following carb cycling

And much more.

You can check out my <u>Ketogenic Diet Books fan page shop</u> for more of the books, as I continue publishing more and more. If you want me to add your category of the Ketogenic diet books that I have published so far, make sure to send me a message. I will do the heavy lifting for you and get back to you with a book that you will love.

You could also subscribe to my newsletter to receive updates whenever I have something new: <u>http://bit.ly/2Cketodietfanton</u>.

Note about nutritional Information per Serving: The carb amounts indicated are net carbs i.e. **total carbs minus dietary fiber**.

Chapter 1: Chocolate Fat Bombs

Cream Cheese Dark Chocolate Keto Fudge

Prep time: 5 min

Cook time: 10 min

Total time: 15 min

Yields: 16 servings

Ingredients

1 teaspoon of vanilla extract

1/3 cup of unsweetened cocoa powder

1 teaspoon of stevia concentrated powder

1 cup of swerve or Sukrin Melis (low carb powdered)

8 ounces of cream cheese

1 cup of unsweetened almond butter or sun butter (nut free) or peanut butter

1 ounce of unsweetened baking chocolate

1 cup of butter

Directions

Fat Bombs

Prepare an 8x8 baking pan by lining it with parchment paper.

Melt the baking chocolate together with the butter over medium heat.

Add the almond butter (or sun butter/peanut butter) and blend in using an electric mixer.

Blend in the cream cheese using the electric mixer.

Remove the cream cheese mixture from heat and stir in the rest of the dry ingredients. Blend with the electric mixer to combine as much as possible then add in the vanilla extract and blend.

Spread the mixture evenly onto the earlier prepared pan then chill in the refrigerator until set.

Nutritional info per serving: Calories 259, Proteins 4g, Carbs 5g and Fat 26g

Fudgy Macadamia Chocolate Fat Bomb

Prep time: 5 minutes

Cook time: 0 minutes

Total time: 5 minutes

Yields: 6 servings

Ingredients

¼ cup of coconut oil or heavy cream

112g (4 oz.) chopped macadamias

2 tablespoons of Swerve

2 tablespoons of unsweetened cocoa powder

58g (2 oz.) cocoa butter

Directions

In a small saucepan, melt the cocoa butter in a bath of water

Add the cocoa powder to the melted butter then add the swerve and mix well until the ingredients are melted and well blended.

Add the macadamias and stir them in well.

Add the coconut oil or the heavy cream and mix well then bring back to room temperature.

Pour the mixture in paper candy cups or molds and leave to cool before placing in fridge to harden.

Nutritional info per serving: Calories 267, Proteins 3g, Carbs 3g and Fats 28g

Low Carb Pecan Fudge Fat Bombs

Prep time: 10 minutes

Cook time: 0 minutes

Total time: 10 minutes

Yields: 10 servings

Ingredients

½ cup of pecans, chopped roughly

1/3 cup of heavy cream

4 tablespoons of Swerve

4 tablespoons of unsweetened cocoa powder

½ cup of coconut oil

4 oz. cocoa powder, food grade

Silicone molds

Directions

Melt the coconut oil and the cocoa butter over a double boiler.

Add the cocoa powder and whisk until there are no clumps.

Pour the mixture into a blender and add the swerve then blend for 1-2 minutes.

Add the heavy cream and blend for around 5 minutes. This will ensure that the sugar dissolves.

Place the silicone molds on a sheet pan and fill them halfway through with pecans.

Pour the mixture into the molds and chill for 4 hours in the refrigerator.

Pop the fat bombs out of the molds and enjoy.

Nutritional info per serving: Calories 140, Proteins 2g, Carbs 3g and Fat 15.3g

Keto Easter Egg Cookie Dough Fat Bombs

Prep time: 30 min

Cook time: 20 min

Total time: 50 min

Yields: 14 servings

Ingredients

1/3 cup (235g) of sugar free dark chocolate chips

¼ teaspoon of gray sea salt

5-10 drops of alcohol free stevia

1 teaspoon of alcohol free vanilla extract

½ cup of coconut oil

2 (70g) of almond flour

Coating

Easter themed natural food coloring

½ cup (112g) of coconut butter, melted

Directions

Line a large baking sheet with silicon baking mat or parchment paper

Add the stevia, vanilla, salt, coconut oil and almond flour to a food processor with an "s" blade and process for about 20 seconds until smooth.

Fold in the sugar-free chocolate chips. Scoop out 1.5 tablespoons of the mixture and roll into a ball in between your palms. Place on the earlier prepared baking sheet and flatten to the shape of a large egg. Repeat this procedure with the remaining dough.

Place the baking sheet in the freezer to chill for an hour.

Prepare a cooling rack by placing it over the top of another separate baking sheet and set aside.

Making the frosting

Melt the coconut butter and divide into separate dishes then add the Easter egg themed food coloring.

Once the cookie dough eggs are ready, remove from freezer. Dip only 1 side of each cookie dough egg into the melted coconut butter and place on the earlier prepared cooling rack.

Add the colored coconut butter to a Ziploc bag then cut out the tip and sprinkle over the top of the "eggs".

Transfer the cooling rack with the colored eggs to the refrigerator and leave to set for 1 hour.

You can store them in a sealed container in the fridge for up to 5 days or freeze them and enjoy for a month.

Nutritional info per serving: Calories 161, Proteins 1.8g, Carbs 5.8g and Fats 15.9g

Keto Chocolate Chip Fat Bombs

Prep time: 10 minutes

Cook time: 10 minutes

Inactive: 1 hour

Total time: 1 hour 20 minutes

Yields: 9 servings

Ingredients

¼ cup of sugar free chocolate chips

¾ cup of heavy cream or coconut milk

½ teaspoon of vanilla extract

¼ teaspoon of sea salt

½ cup of grass fed butter or coconut oil or ghee, melted

¼ cup of swerve

Directions

In a large bowl, combine the coconut flour, vanilla, butter, salt, swerve and heavy cream (or coconut milk) until well blended.

Fold in the chocolate chips.

Place in the refrigerator to set for 1 hour.

Remove from fridge and roll into balls.

Place in a container to store in the freezer and enjoy one at a time.

Nutritional info per serving: Calories 165, Proteins 1.1g, Carbs 6.7g and Fat 5.2g

Easy Chocolate Fat Bombs with Coconut Oil

Prep time: 10 minutes

Cook time: 0 minutes

Total time: 10 minutes

Yields: 20 servings

Ingredients

¼ cup of cocoa powder

1/3 cup of powdered monk fruit sweetener

2 tablespoons of coconut oil, measured in solid form then melted

2 tablespoons of MCT oil (or more coconut oil)

2 cups of macadamia nuts, roasted dry and salted

Optional:

1 teaspoon of vanilla extract

Directions

Puree/pulse the macadamia nuts in a food processor or a high power blender until the nuts are mostly broken down into small bits.

Add the vanilla, melted coconut oil and MCT oil then continue to blend until you form nut butter – try to get the butter smooth but it's also fine if you can't get rid of stray pieces. Scrape down the nuts on the sides if any.

Fat Bombs

Gradually add the sweetener and the cacao powder, a few tablespoons at a time and puree after every addition until smooth

Prepare a mini muffin pan by lining it with parchment liners. Spoon or pour the batter onto each liner evenly until about 1/3 of the way full.

Freeze the chocolate fat bombs until solid for at least 30 minutes.

Nutritional info per serving: Calories 122, Proteins 1g, Carbs 2g and Fats 13g

White Chocolate Fat Bombs

Prep time: 5 minutes

Cook time: 10 minutes

Total time: 15 minutes

Yields: 8 servings

Ingredients

10 drops of vanilla stevia drops

¼ cup (35g) of coconut oil

¼ cup (25g) of cocoa butter

Directions

Place the coconut oil and cocoa butter in a double boiler and melt together over low heat.

Remove from heat then add in the vanilla flavored stevia drops and stir.

Pour the mixture into molds and chill until hardened.

Remove the fat bombs from molds and enjoy.

Store in refrigerator.

Nutritional info per serving: Calories 125, Protein 0g, Carbs 0g and Fat 10g

White Chocolate Raspberry Fat Bombs

Prep time: 5 minutes

Cook time: 0 minutes

Chill time: 1 hour

Total time: 1 hour 5 minutes

Yields: 10-12 fat bombs

Ingredients

1/4 cup of powdered erythritol sweetener (such as Swerve)

1/2 cup of freeze-dried raspberries

2 ounces of cacao butter

1/2 cup of coconut oil

Directions

Prepare a 12-cup muffin pan by lining with paper liners or just use a silicone muffin pan.

In a small pan, heat the cacao butter and the coconut oil over low heat until they completely melt then remove the pan from heat

Place the freeze-dried raspberries in a coffee grinder, blender or food processor and grind.

Add the powdered erythritol and the pulverized berries to the small saucepan and stir until the erythritol is mostly dissolved.

Distribute the mixture evenly among the muffin cups. The berry powder will sink to the bottom of the muffin pan – no worry. Just ensure that as you pour the mixture into each mold, you stir it first so that each gets some raspberry powder.

Chill until firm for 1 hour. You can store in the refrigerator for several weeks.

Nutritional info per serving: Calories 153, Proteins 0.2g, Carbs 1.2g and Fats 16.6g

Chocolate Cherry Fat Bombs

Prep time: 10 minutes

Cook time: 0 minutes

Chill time: 1 hour

Total time: 1 hour 10 minutes

Yields: 12 fat bombs

Ingredients

¾ cup of frozen dark sweet cherries, thawed

½ teaspoon of vanilla extract

½ teaspoon of almond extract

5 drops of stevia

3 tablespoons of cacao powder

¼ cup of cocoa butter, melted

¼ cup of coconut oil, melted

Directions

Mix all ingredients apart from the dark berries.

Mash the dark cherries with a fork once they have thawed then mix them together with their juices in the chocolate mix.

Use a tablespoon to spoon a tablespoonful into an ice cube tray or mini cupcake liners. Freeze for 1 hour or longer.

Store in the fridge.

Nutritional info per serving: Calories 67, Proteins 0g, Carbs 2g and Fat 6g

Chapter 2: Mocha Fat Bombs

Perfect Keto Mocha Fat Bombs

Prep time: 10 minutes

Cook time: 0 minutes

Total time: 10 minutes

Yields: 24 fat bombs

Ingredients

1 scoop MCT Oil Powder

2 tablespoons of monk fruit sweetener

2 tablespoons of heavy whipping cream

4 tablespoons of coconut oil

2 shots of espresso

3 oz. of cream cheese, softened

5 tablespoons of unsalted Kerrygold butter, softened

1/2 scoop of Perfect Keto Chocolate Sea Salt Ketone Supplement

Directions

Melt together the heavy whipping cream, coconut oil, espresso, cream cheese and butter in a double boiler.

Remove from heat then add the rest of the ingredients.

Mix all ingredients with a hand mixer until well combined.

Spoon the mixture into your silicone mold then freeze for about 4 hours.

Remove from the fat bombs from your silicone mold after they have frozen and enjoy.

Nutritional info per serving: Calories 63, Proteins 0.3g, Carbs 1.3g and Fat 6.8g

Keto Mocha Latte Fat Bomb Bars

Prep time: 10 minutes

Cook time: 0 minutes

Total time: 10 minutes

Yields: 16 servings

Ingredients

2 tablespoons of unsweetened cocoa powder

1 tablespoon of hot water, filtered

1 teaspoon of espresso powder

¼ cup of organic heavy cream, grass-fed – ideally raw

2 teaspoons of organic vanilla extract

½ cup of Monk fruit sweetener

1 cup of organic grass-fed butter or if you prefer ghee

18 ounces of organic cultured cream cheese

Directions

In a large bowl, combine the heavy cream, vanilla, Monk fruit sweetener, butter and cream cheese and beat/whip using a stand or hand mixer until smooth.

Scoop out roughly ½ of the mixture and set aside.

Add instant coffee to hot water to dissolve.

To half of the mixture remaining in the mixing bowl, add the cocoa and the now dissolved coffee. Beat until well combined.

In a regular pan lined with wax paper or an 8x8 (or a similar sized) silicone pan, pour the mocha layer at the bottom and spread evenly. Top with the vanilla layer.

Freeze until solid or overnight.

Remove from pan then use a large knife dipped in hot water to cut into 16 pieces.

Store in an airtight container in the freezer for up to a month.

Nutritional info per serving: Calories 148, Proteins 2g, Carbs 1g and Fats 15g

Peppermint Mocha Fat Bombs

Prep time: 5 minutes

Cook time: 0 minutes

Total time: 5 minutes

Yields: 16 servings

Ingredients

5-8 drops of liquid stevia

2 teaspoons of instant coffee powder

2 tablespoons of organic cocoa powder

¼ teaspoon of peppermint extract

3 tablespoons of hemp seeds

3 tablespoons of coconut oil, melted

¾ cup of coconut butter, melted

Directions

Mix together the peppermint extract, hemp seeds, 1 tablespoon of coconut oil and melted coconut butter.

Pour the mixture into molds to about ¾ of the way.

Refrigerate until firm.

Stir together the stevia, instant coffee, cocoa powder and 2 tablespoons of melted coconut oil then sprinkle on the fat bombs.

Place back in the refrigerator until they completely harden

Pop the fat bombs out of the molds then transfer to an airtight container and store in the freezer or fridge.

Nutritional info per serving: Calories 121, Proteins 2g, Carbs 4g and Fat 11g

Keto Matcha MCT Fat Bombs

Prep time: 2 minutes

Cook time: 3 minutes

Total time: 4 hours 5 minutes

Yields: 24 fat bombs

Ingredients

½ teaspoon of cinnamon

1 scoop of keto perfect Matcha MCT oil powder

2 tablespoons of softened cream cheese

2 tablespoons of coconut oil

½ cup of raw cocoa butter

1/4 cup HWC

Directions

Place the cocoa butter in the microwave and heat in 30 second increments, until just melted – stir each time during the increments.

Add all ingredients to a mixing bowl and mix using a hand mixer until the ingredients are well combined.

Spoon the mixture quickly into silicon molds then place flat in the freezer. Freeze for about 4 hours until solid.

Pop the fat bombs out of the silicone molds and enjoy.

Nutritional info per serving: Calories 65, Protein 0.1g, Carbs 0.2g and Fats 7.5g

Bulletproof Fat Bombs

Prep time: 15 minutes

Cook time: 30-60 minutes

Inactive: 2-3 hours

Total time: 3-4 hours

Yields: 20 servings

Ingredients

¼ cup (2 oz. /56g) of extra virgin coconut oil or grass-fed butter

¼ cup (1.4 oz. /40g) of powdered Swerve or Erythritol

10-15 drops of liquid stevia extract

2 tablespoons of raw cocoa powder, unsweetened

2 tablespoons of brain octane oil or MCT oil or more coconut oil

1 cup (8.8 oz. /250g) full-fat cream cheese or mascarpone cheese or creamed coconut milk

½ cup 4 oz. /120 Ml) of strong brewed coffee or chicory coffee (caffeine-free)

Optional:

1 teaspoon of rum extract

Directions

Place the cocoa powder, MCT oil, coconut oil (or butter) and the softened full fat cream cheese (or mascarpone cheese).

Add the stevia and erythritol into a blender and blend till smooth.

Add the prepared coffee (lukewarm or room temp, not hot) into the blender with the stevia mixture and blend again until smooth.

Pour the coffee mixture into an ice-cream maker and process according the instructions on the manual – takes 30 to 60 minutes depending on the type of ice-cream maker you have. An ice cream maker makes the mixture creamy and the texture smoother.

If you don't have an ice cream maker: pour the mixture directly into a small muffin tin or an ice tray. Use 2 tablespoons for each fat bomb or make them smaller. Also, instead of using ½ cup of coffee, you can use 1-2 teaspoons of instant coffee powder. The mixture will turn out thick enough so you will not need an ice cream maker.

Scoop about 2 tablespoons of the mixture into an ice tray which is perfect for making fat bomb shapes.

Place in the freezer until firm for 2-3 hours.

Nutritional info per serving: Calories77, Protein 0.8g, Carbs 0.7g and Fat 8.1g

Chapter 3: Coconut Fat Bombs

Coconut And Cinnamon Keto Fat Bomb

Prep time: 1 hour 30 minutes

Cook time: 10 minutes

Total time: 1 hour 40 minutes

Yields: 10 balls

Ingredients

1 cup of coconut shreds

1 teaspoon of cinnamon

1 teaspoon of nutmeg

1 teaspoon of gluten free vanilla extract

1 cup of full fat coconut milk, canned

1 cup of coconut butter or almond butter

1 teaspoon of stevia powder extract or according to your preferred taste

Directions

If you don't have a double boiler, place a glass bowl inside a saucepan with few inches of water to make a double boiler.

Add all ingredients apart from the shredded coconut to your double boiler over medium heat.

Stir the ingredients while you wait for them to melt.

Remove the bowl from heat once all ingredients are combined.

Put the bowl in the fridge until the mixture is hard enough to be rolled into balls – takes about 30 minutes.

Roll the mixture into 1 inch balls then roll them in the coconut shreds.

Put the balls on a plate then refrigerate for an hour.

Enjoy.

*If you are not serving, keep refrigerated

Nutritional info per serving: Calories 341, Protein 3.3g, Carbs 12.8g and Fat 31.9g

Strawberry-Filled Coconut Fat Bombs

Prep time: 5 minutes

Cook time: 5 minutes

Total time: 10 minutes

Yields: 15 fat bombs

Ingredients

1 tablespoon of unsweetened shredded coconut

1/3 cup (about 75g) of fresh strawberries, diced

8-10 drops of liquid stevia, to taste

½ tablespoon of cocoa powder

1/3 cup of coconut oil + 1 tablespoon

1/3 cup of coconut butter

Directions

In a bain-marie, add a few drops of liquid stevia, cocoa powder, 1/3 cup of coconut oil and coconut butter then heat until fully melted

Meanwhile, add a few spoonful's of water and fresh strawberries to a small frying pan and cook until soft, over medium heat. Mash the berries with a fork then place them in a blender with a few more drops of liquid stevia and a tablespoon of melted coconut oil.

Pour the melted coconut mixture into molds then add about a teaspoon of the strawberry mixture in each mold. Sprinkle the top with a few shreds of the unsweetened coconut.

Place the mold in the refrigerator to fully harden for at least a couple of hours or preferably overnight.

Pop the fat bombs out of the molds then place in an airtight container and store in the fridge.

Nutritional info per serving: Calories 106, Proteins 1g, Carbs 2g and Fat 11g

Blackberry Coconut Fat Bomb

Prep time: 5 minutes

Cook time: 5 minutes

Total time: 10 minutes

Yields: 16 small squares

Ingredients

1 tablespoon of lemon juice

½ teaspoon of vanilla extract or ¼ teaspoon of vanilla powder

½ a teaspoon of SweetLeaf stevia drops or more for sweeter taste

½ cup of frozen or fresh blackberries (you can use raspberries or strawberries if desired)

1 cup of coconut oil

1 cup of coconut butter

Directions

Place the blackberries (if frozen), coconut oil and coconut butter in a pot and heat until just well combined over medium heat.

In a small blender or food processor, add the remaining ingredients and the coconut mixture prepared above and process until smooth.

Note: if the coconut mixture is too hot, separation may occur. If you are using fresh berries, you don't need to cook them with the coconut butter and oil.

Spread out the batter onto a small pan lined with parchment paper then refrigerate until the mixture hardens for 1 hour.

Remove from pan and cut into small squares.

If you are not eating the fat bombs immediately or if you have leftovers, store them, covered, in the refrigerator.

Nutritional info per serving: Calories 170, Proteins 1.1g, Carbs 3g and Fat 18.7g

Keto Chocolate Coconut Fat Bombs

Prep time: 5 minutes

Cook time: 0 minutes

Inactive: 25 minutes

Total time: 30 minutes

Yields: 30 servings

Ingredients

1 teaspoon of vanilla

2 tablespoons of powdered Swerve sweetener

1 stick (1/2 cup) of butter

1 cup of Lily's chocolate chips, melted

1 cup of coconut oil

4 cups of unsweetened coconut flakes

Directions

Melt the butter and coconut oil.

Combine the coconut flakes and the melted coconut oil and butter in a medium bowl.

Add the vanilla to mixture and mix until fully combined.

Sprinkle the powdered swerve sweetener on mixture and mix again until it is fully incorporated.

Prepare a square pan by layering a piece of parchment paper at the bottom.

Pour the coconut mixture into the prepared pan then place in the freezer to set for about 5 minutes.

Remove the coconut mix from the freezer then pour the melted chocolate on top and spread evenly.

Return the mixture to the freezer and leave to set completely for about 10 to 20 minutes.

Remove pan from freezer then remove the parchment paper with the fat bombs and place on a flat surface.

Cut into squares with a sharp knife.

Nutritional info per serving: Calories 119, Protein 0.3g, Carbs 1.2g and Fat 12.8g

Triple Layer Coconut Almond Butter Cups

Prep time: 5 minutes

Cook time: 2 minutes

Inactive: 1 hour 15 minutes

Total time: 1 hour 22 minutes

Yields: 12 cups

Ingredients

Bottom layer:

2-3 drops of pure almond extract

¼ teaspoon of ground Ceylon cinnamon

1 teaspoon of vanilla powder

¼ cup of coconut oil

½ cup of cacao paste, chopped finely

Middle layer:

¼ teaspoon of ground Ceylon cinnamon

¼ cup of coconut oil

½ cup of all natural almond butter

Top layer:

½ cup of creamy coconut butter

¼ cup of coconut oil

Garnish:

Toasted coconut flakes

Whole raw almonds

Directions

Line a muffin pan with silicone cups or large parchment paper.

Melt ¾ cup of the coconut oil using your preferred method (this is if it is not already in liquid state).

Use a small mixing bowl (preferably one equipped with a spout) to melt the cacao paste in your microwave stirring in 20-30 second intervals until there are no lumps left. Stir in the almond extract, vanilla powder, cinnamon and ¼ cup of the melted coconut oil. Mix well until completely combined.

Distribute the melted chocolate evenly between the 12 muffin cups then place in fridge for about 5 minutes to set.

Meanwhile, in a separate mixing bowl, add ¼ cup of the melted coconut oil, ground cinnamon and almond butter and stir to combine. Pour this mixture over the now set chocolate then place back in the refrigerator for about 5-10 minutes until this new layer sets.

Meanwhile, as the cups are setting, add ½ cup of the creamy coconut butter to the bowl that you had melted the coconut oil in (it should have ¼ cup of the oil remaining) and stir until well combined.

Spoon the above mixture delicately over the almond butter layer and garnish each cup with whole almond or a pinch of toasted coconut flakes.

Place the cups back in the refrigerator for at least an hour to finish setting.

You can keep the cups for several weeks if stored in an airtight container in the fridge

Nutritional info per serving: Calories 180, Protein 3g, Carbs 1g and Fat 15g

Tropical Coconut Key Lime Pie Fat Bombs

Prep time: 5 minutes

Cook time: 0 minutes

Total time: 25 to 35 minutes

Yields: 18 fat bombs

Ingredients

1/3 cup of stevia or any other keto friendly sweetener of your choice

1 cup of almond flour

1/3 cup of coconut flour

2 scoops of Perfect Keto vanilla collagen

6 tablespoons of coconut oil

½ cup of coconut butter, melted

2 teaspoons of key or regular lime zest

½ cup of key or regular lime juice

Optional:

½ cup of shredded coconut flakes, unsweetened (plain or toasted until golden brown

Directions

Place all ingredients in a food processor and process on high until smooth.

Divide, shape into fat bombs and place on a tray, wire rack or a lined baking sheet and freeze or refrigerate until set for 20 to 30 minutes.

Nutritional info per serving: Calories 114, Proteins 3g, Carbs 3g and Fat 11g

Keto Butter Coconut Bites

Prep time: 10 minutes

Cook time: 0 minutes

Freeze time: 80 minutes

Total time: 90 minutes

Yields: 6 servings

Ingredients

1/3 cup coconut butter

¼ cup coconut oil

4 tablespoons of Perfect Keto butter

1 scoop of Perfect Keto chocolate collagen

Directions

Melt the coconut oil then mix it in a bowl with Perfect Keto chocolate collagen.

Distribute the chocolate mixture evenly among 6 muffin tins and freeze for 10 minutes.

Remove from freezer and spoon the base evenly with softened coconut butter then place back in the freezer for 10 more minutes.

Remove from freezer and spoon each frozen coconut bite evenly with Perfect Keto chocolate butter.

Freeze again for at least 1 hour.

Nutritional info per serving: Calories 120, Protein 3g, Carbs 0.8g and Fat 26g

Coconut Lemon Fat Bombs

Prep time: 5 minutes

Cook time: 0 minutes

Chill time: 70 minutes

Total time: 75 minutes

Yields: 5 fat bombs

Ingredients

1 teaspoon of granulated monk fruit sweetener

1/3 cup of coconut oil

1/3 cup of softened coconut butter

1 scoop of Perfect Keto Greens powder lemons

Directions

Place all ingredients in a bowl and mix until dissolved.

Pour the mixture into muffin trays then place in the freezer for not less than 1 hour.

Enjoy!

Nutritional info per serving: Calories 211, Protein 0.2g, Carbs 0g and Fat 23.6g

Chocolate Coconut Almond Fat Bombs

Prep time: 10 minutes

Cook time: 50 minutes

Total time: 1 hour

Yields: 30 servings

Ingredients

¼ cup of cacao nibs

¼ cup of finely shredded coconut, unsweetened

¼ cup of crushed sliced almonds

½ teaspoon of erythritol or 10 drops of stevia

½ teaspoon of vanilla extract

1 teaspoon of almond extract

¼ cup of cocoa powder or cacao powder

½ cup of melted coconut butter

½ cup of melted coconut oil

Directions

Mix together the erythritol (or stevia), vanilla extract, almond extract, cacao powder, coconut butter and coconut oil.

If you are using erythritol: heat on the stove or in the microwave until it is dissolved for 1-2 minutes. You are recommended to taste in order to ensure that there are no crunchy erythritol crystals.

Add the cacao nibs, coconut flakes and crushed slivered almonds. Fill an ice cube tray or mini cupcake liners using a tablespoon with 1 tablespoon full in each.

Store in the fridge.

Nutritional info per serving: Calories 72, Protein 0g, Carbs 1g and Fat 7g

Coconut Ginger Fat Bomb

Prep time: 5 minutes

Cook time: 0 minutes

Total time: 5 minutes

Yields: 10 servings

Ingredients

1 teaspoon of ginger

1 teaspoon of granulated sweetener of your choice (or more according to your taste)

25g of shredded/desiccated coconut, unsweetened

75g of softened coconut oil

75g of softened coconut butter

Directions

Add all ingredients to a pouring jug and mix until the sweetener is dissolved.

Pour into ice block trays or silicon molds and refrigerate for a minimum of 10 minutes.

Nutritional info per serving: Calories 120, Protein 0.5g, Carbs 2.2, Fat 12.8g

Nutty Coconut Fat Bombs

Prep time: 15 minutes

Cook time: 0 minutes

Total time: 15 minutes

Yields: 15 servings

Ingredients

2 tablespoons of cacao nibs

¼ teaspoon of kosher salt

½ teaspoon of vanilla bean powder

1 teaspoon of cinnamon

2 tablespoons of hemp seeds

2 tablespoons of flax meal

2 tablespoons of chia seeds

2 tablespoons of almond butter or any other nut butter of your choice

¼ cup of coconut butter plus 1 extra tablespoon if needed

½ cup of shredded coconut

1 ½ cup of walnuts or any other nut of your choice

Optional: maple syrup

For the chocolate drizzle:

½ teaspoon of coconut oil

1 oz. unsweetened or bittersweet chocolate, chopped

Directions

Combine all ingredients apart from the cacao nibs in the bowl of a food processor and pulse until the mixture starts to break down for about 1-2 minutes - the mixture will first of all become powdery and stick together but will still be crumbly

Continue processing until the oils begin to release a bit and the mixture easily sticks together – just ensure you are careful enough to not over process; otherwise, you will have nut butter.

If you are not using maple syrup or if your mixture seems dry, you will need one more tablespoon of coconut butter for the mixture come together. Quickly pulse cacao nibs to incorporate them once the mixture sticks together well.

Use a tablespoon scoop or a small cookie scoop to distribute the mixture equally into pieces. Roll the mixture into balls with your hands then place on a plate.

If you want the chocolate drizzle, make it by melting together the coconut oil and the chocolate in the microwave until completely melted for 30 seconds to 1 minute.

Drizzle the chocolate over the balls then place in the freezer or fridge to firm up

Store in a zip-lock bag or an airtight container in the freezer or refrigerator.

* Nutritional info does not include maple syrup and chocolate drizzle.

Nutritional info per serving: Calories 164, Protein 4g, Carbs 6g and Fat 14g

Chapter 4: Nutty Fat Bombs

Chocolate Walnut Keto Fat Bombs

Prep time: 5 minutes

Cook time: 0 minutes

Freeze time: 25 minutes

Total time: 30 minutes

Yields: 30 servings

Ingredients

8 drops of stevia

1 teaspoon of cinnamon

1/3 cup (50g) of small walnut pieces

¼ cup (55g) of coconut oil

3.5 ounces (100g) of dark chocolate, min. 85% cocoa solids

Directions

Melt the coconut oil and the chocolate in a water bath in a coated pot over gentle heat on the stove or in a microwave in 4x30 second bursts. If you are using unsweetened chocolate, add 2 tablespoons of powdered erythritol sweetener.

Place the walnuts in a food processor and process until you have small pieces. Keep a few larger walnut pieces to decorate the fat bombs.

Optional step: dry roast the walnuts over low heat until browned.

Add stevia, cinnamon and the crushed walnuts to the coconut oil/chocolate mixture then pour the resulting mix into an ice cube tray or silicone molds and freeze until the tops are just set for about 5 minutes.

Remove molds from freezer then place the larger walnut pieces on top. Place the fat bombs in the fridge until they set for another 20 minutes or more.

Nutritional info per serving: Calories 46, Proteins 0.3g, Carbs 0.7g and Fats 4.8g

Sugar-Free Keto Peanut Butter Cups

Prep time: 10 minutes

Cook time: 5 minutes

Inactive: 50 minutes

Total time: 1 hour 5 minutes

Yields:

Ingredients

For chocolate layer:

5 tablespoons of coconut oil, divided

10 oz. of sugar free dark chocolate

Optional: ½ teaspoon of vanilla extract (divided)

For peanut butter layer:

1 ½ teaspoon of peanut flour

2 teaspoons of coconut oil

3 ½ tablespoons of creamy peanut butter

4 teaspoons of powdered erythritol (to taste)

Optional:

1/8 teaspoon of vanilla extract (to taste)

1 pinch of sea salt (to taste)

Directions

Prepare a muffin pan by lining it with candy cups or parchment liners.

For the bottom chocolate layer: heat half of the coconut oil (35g/2 ½ tablespoons) and half of the chocolate (142g/ 5 oz.) on the stove in a double boiler, stirring frequently until completely melted. (You can also melt in the microwave stirring at 20 sec intervals.) If using the vanilla extract, stir in half (¼ teaspoon) of it.

Fill the parchment cups or candy cups evenly with the chocolate (about 10 Ml/ 2 teaspoons in each.) Place in the freezer until the top is firm for 10 minutes.

For the peanut butter layer: heat the coconut oil and the peanut butter in a double boiler or in the microwave as done earlier with the chocolate. Stir in the vanilla (if using), peanut flour, sea salt (if using) and powdered sweetener until smooth then adjust the salt and sweetener to taste according to your desire.

In each cup half filled with the chocolate layer, add a teaspoon of the peanut butter mixture at the center of the cups. The peanut butter mixture will spread a little to form a circle that will not quite reach the edges. Freeze for 10 more minutes until the top is firm.

As the chocolate peanut butter mixture is freezing, make the top chocolate layer. Heat the remaining coconut oil (35g/ 2 ½ tablespoons) and the remaining chocolate (142g / 5oz.) in a microwave or double boiler as explained earlier. Stir in the remaining vanilla extract (¼ teaspoon), if using.

Remove the chocolate-peanut butter mixture from the freezer then pour the chocolate on top of the peanut butter layer – about 10 Ml (2 teaspoons) in each. The chocolate will fill the sides of the peanut butter circles and cover the top as well.

Return to the freezer until completely firm for at least 20-30 minutes. Store in the refrigerator.

Nutritional info per serving: Calories 187, Protein 3g, Carbs 3g and Fat 18g

White Chocolate Peanut Butter Fat Bombs

Prep time: 5 minutes

Cook time: 5 minutes

Total time: 10 minutes

Yields: 20+ fat bombs depending on your mold size

Ingredients

1-2 teaspoons of honey or maple syrup (more or less to taste)

1 teaspoon of vanilla extract or paste

2 tablespoons of full fat coconut milk

1 ½ tablespoons of coconut oil

¼ cup of almond or peanut butter (sugar-free)

¼ teaspoon of sea salt – less if the peanut butter is salted

120g of cocoa butter (approx. 1 cup)

Optional: a few drops of stevia to taste

Directions

Add the coconut milk, peanut butter, coconut oil and cocoa butter to a double boiler or a small saucepan over very low heat and heat until just melted. Whisk the ingredients well to combine then turn off heat.

Remove the pan from heat then stir in the sweetener of your choice and vanilla to taste. Add sea salt to taste.

Pour the mixture into your molds and place in the freezer to set for about 30-60 minutes.

Enjoy immediately you remove from freezer or refrigerator – storing at room temperature will make it too melty.

Nutritional info per serving: Calories 40, Protein 3g, Carbs 1g and Fat 12g

Chocolate Sea Salt Peanut Butter Bites

Prep time: 10 minutes

Cook time:

Total time: 4 hours 10 minutes

Yields: 30 servings

Ingredients

2 teaspoons of coarse sea salt

1 tablespoon of Swerve

1 teaspoon of vanilla extract

1 tablespoon of heavy cream

¾ cup of butter

8 oz. of cream cheese

1 cup of unsweetened peanut butter

1 scoop of perfect keto chocolate sea salt, exogenous ketone supplement

Directions

Prepare an 8×8 baking pan by lining it with parchment paper.

Melt the butter, cream cheese and peanut butter in a medium saucepan over medium heat and stir until well combined.

Remove mixture from heat and set aside.

Add the perfect keto chocolate sea salt, Swerve, vanilla extract and heavy cream to a large mixing bowl then pour in the peanut butter mixture. Using a hand mixer, mix until smooth.

Pour the fudge into the earlier prepared baking pan and spread evenly. Sprinkle the top with coarse sea salt.

Chill the fudge in the refrigerator for at least 4 hours or preferably overnight.

Nutritional info per serving: Calories 122, Proteins 2.9g, Carbs 1.9g and Fat 11.3g

Almond Pistachio Fat Bombs

Prep time: 10 minutes

Cook time: 0 minutes

Total time: 10 minutes

Yields: 36 pieces

Ingredients

¼ cup of raw shelled pistachios, chopped

¼ teaspoon of Himalayan salt

¼ teaspoon of pure almond extract

2 teaspoons of chai spice

1 tablespoon of pure vanilla extract

¼ cup of ghee

½ cup of full fat coconut milk, chilled overnight

1 cup of firm coconut oil

1 cup of creamy coconut butter

1 cup of all natural almonds, roasted

½ cup of cacao butter, chopped finely and melted

Directions

Grease a 9" square baking pan and line it with parchment paper leaving a little hanging on both sides for easy unmolding once done cooking. Set aside.

In a small saucepan, melt the cacao butter over low heat or place in microwave and stir often regardless of the option you choose. Reserve.

In a large mixing bowl, add all ingredients apart from the shelled pistachios and cacao butter and mix using a hand mixer starting on low speed and progressing to high until all ingredients are fully combined and the mixture is airy and light.

Add the melted cacao butter into the almond mixture and proceed mixing on low speed until it is fully incorporated.

Pour the mixture onto the earlier prepared pan and spread as evenly as you can then sprinkle the top with the chopped pistachios.

Refrigerate until it's completely set for at least 4 hours (but its better refrigerated overnight).

Cut into 36 squares and enjoy.

Nutritional info per serving: Calories 130, Protein 3g, Carbs 0.8g and Fat 14g

Macadamia Nut Fat Bombs

Prep time: 20 minutes

Cook time: 20 minutes

Total time: 40 minutes

Yields: 6 servings

Ingredients

12 macadamia nuts

1 teaspoon of vanilla extract

2 tablespoons of erythritol or swerve

2 tablespoons of unsweetened cocoa powder

1/3 cup of unrefined coconut oil (at room temp)

Pinch of salt

Directions

Whisk together the vanilla extract erythritol (or swerve), vanilla and coconut oil in a small bowl until smooth

Prepare a small container by lining it with parchment paper then pour in the chocolate mix. Spread the chocolate at the bottom thinly and evenly using a spatula.

Add the macadamia nuts to the chocolate mixture. You can make fun shapes or be really systematic.

Sprinkle the salt lightly all over the mix then place the container in the freezer to set for 20 minutes. Remove from freezer and cut evenly into 6 squares.

Store in the freezer.

Nutritional info per serving: Calories 99, Protein 0.8g, Carbs 1.9g and Fat 16.9g

Pecan Pie Fudge Bombs

Prep time: 5 minutes

Cook time: 5 minutes

Chill time: 1-2 hours

Total time: 1-2 hours

Yields: 12 servings

Ingredients

½ cup of chopped pecans

1 tablespoon of cacao powder

2 tablespoons of golden Lakanto, swerve or any keto friendly sweetener of choice

2 tablespoons of grass fed butter

¼ cup of sugar free chocolate chips or 2 pieces of 100% cacao

½ cup of cacao butter

½ cup of coconut butter

Directions

Place the pecans in a small pot and toast for 3 to 5 minutes under low heat just until fragrant and lightly golden brown. Remove from heat and leave to cool then chop roughly and set aside.

Add the rest of the ingredients to the pot and melt over low heat until smooth. Stir in the chopped pecans and adjust the sweetener if need be.

Remove mixture from heat then pour into silicone molds.

Place the molds in the freezer until firm for 1 to 2 hours

Nutritional info per serving: Calories 163, Proteins 3g, Carbs 2g and Fats 18g

Keto Salted Almond Bourbon Truffle Fat Bombs

Prep time: 2 minutes

Cook time: 0 minutes

Chill time: 1 hour

Total time: 1 hour 2 minutes

Yields: 15 servings

Ingredients

¾ cup of roasted and salted almonds chopped

1 teaspoon of organic vanilla extract

2 tablespoons of heavy cream or organic coconut cream

2 tablespoons of monk fruit sweetener

2 tablespoons of organic expeller pressed coconut oil

2 tablespoons of Maker's Mark bourbon

3 scoops of MCT powder

½ cup of cocoa powder

2 medium avocados

1 pinch of sea salt

Directions

Combine all ingredients apart from the almonds in your blender or food processor and process until smooth.

Transfer to a bowl and chill for 1 hour in the refrigerator.

Scoop the chilled truffles using a cookie dough scooper then roll in the chopped almonds.

Store the fat bombs in the freezer or refrigerator. You can keep it for up to 2 weeks.

Nutritional info per serving: Calories 111, Protein 2g, Carbs 6g and Fat 10g

Low Carb Almond Granola

Prep time: 1 minute

Cook time: 15 minutes

Total time: 16 minutes

Yields: 16 servings

Ingredients

¼ cup of natural peanut butter

1 teaspoon of pumpkin pie spice

¼ cup of coconut butter

1 large egg

2 tablespoons of vanilla extract

1 cup of unsweetened coconut flakes

1 cup of sunflower seeds

1 cup of almonds

½ cup of sugar-free dark chocolate chips

1 cup of high quality macadamia nuts

Directions

Preheat your oven to 350 degrees F.

Place everything in a blender and blend for a few seconds until the ingredients are blended.

Press the mixture into a shallow glass baking dish such as a shallow pie baking dish.

Bake until it starts to brown at the top for around 15 minutes.

Cut and enjoy.

Nutritional info per serving: Calories 202, Protein 5g, Carbs 6g and Fat 19g

Easy Almond Butter Fat Bombs

Prep time: 5 minutes

Cook time: 0 minutes

Total time: 5 minutes

Yields: 6 servings

Ingredients

¼ cup of powdered swerve

2 tablespoons of cacao powder

¼ cup of unrefined coconut oil

¼ cup of almond butter

Directions

In a medium bowl, mix together the coconut oil and the almond butter.

Microwave for around 30-45 seconds then stir until smooth.

Stir in the cacao powder and the swerve.

Pour into silicone molds and refrigerate until firm.

Nutritional info per serving: Calories 189, Protein 3.2g, Carbs3.6g and Fat 19.1g

Lemon Macadamia Fat Bombs

Prep time: 3 minutes

Cook time: 2 minutes

Total time: 5 minutes

Yields: 30 servings

Ingredients

½ cup of macadamia nuts

½ cup of unsweetened organic shredded coconut

1 medium lemon, zested and juiced

1 splash of organic vanilla extract

3 tablespoons of organic coconut flour

3 tablespoons of Blanched almond flour, superfine

2 ounces of organic coconut cream concentrate

1 ounce of cacao butter

6 ounces of organic Expeller Pressed coconut oil

Liquid stevia to taste

1 pinch of sea salt

Directions

In a small saucepan, melt the cocoa butter, coconut cream concentrate and coconut oil over low heat

Combine the coconut flour, stevia, almond flour, lemon zest/juice, vanilla and the melted mixture in your blender and blend for 1 plus minutes until well combined.

Add the macadamia nuts and the shredded coconut and pulse a few times to combine then lightly chop.

Press into a silicone mold or portion into bite sized balls and freeze until firm. Enjoy refrigerated or frozen.

Chapter 5: Other Fat Bomb Recipes

Easy Vanilla Fat Bombs

Prep time: 10 minutes

Cook time: 30-50 minutes

Total time: 40-60 minutes

Yields: 14 servings

Ingredients

2 teaspoons of vanilla extract (sugar-free) or 1 vanilla bean

¼ cup (2 oz. /55g) of virgin coconut oil

1 cup (4.6 oz. /130g) of unsalted macadamia nuts

¼ cup (2oz. /55g) of butter or more coconut oil

2 tablespoons of Swerve

Optional:

10-15 drops of stevia extract

Directions

Add the macadamia nuts into a blender and blend till smooth.

Mix with the coconut oil (melted in water bath or room temperature) and softened butter.

Add the vanilla extract, stevia and Swerve.

Pour the mixture into an ice cube tray or mini muffin forms. To yield 14 servings, fill each one with about 1 ½ tablespoons of the mixture.

Place in the refrigerator to solidify for at least 30 minutes.

Keep the fat bombs refrigerated as butter and coconut oil get very soft at room temp.

Nutritional info per serving: Calories 132, Proteins 0.79g, Carbs 1.6g and Fats 14.4g

Everything Bagel and Lox Keto Fat Bombs

Prep time: 5 minutes

Cook time: 0 minutes

Chill time: 2-3 hours

Total time: 2-3 hours

Yields: 36 servings

Ingredients

Homemade Everything bagel seasoning

2 medium scallions, thinly sliced

4 ounces of wild caught smoked salmon

8 ounces of organic cultured cream cheese

Directions

Beat the cream cheese using a stand or hand mixer until fluffy.

Add the thinly sliced scallions and the chopped smoked salmon and beat until well incorporated.

Roll the mixture into bite sized balls and then coat lightly in the homemade everything bagel seasoning.

Chill for 2 to 3 hours in order for the flavors to come together and enjoy. You can store them in the fridge for up to a week or freeze for longer storage.

*Allow the fat bombs to thaw in the fridge before you eat them.

You can use finely diced red onions instead of the scallions then add capers if desired.

Ensure you use smoked salmon (raw) and not hot smoked salmon.

Nutritional info per serving: Calories 25, Proteins 1g, Carbs 0.5g and Fats 2g

Pumpkin Pie Fat Bombs

Prep time: 20 minutes

Cook time: 3 minutes

Total time: 23 minutes

Yields: 15 fat bombs

Ingredients

½ cup of pecans

2 teaspoons of pumpkin pie spice

¼ cup of So Nourished erythritol

½ cup of coconut oil

2 oz. of coconut butter

½ cup of pumpkin puree

Directions

If your coconut oil is not already liquid, start off by melting it.

Melt down the coconut butter until it is soft as it is easier to work with.

In a mixing bowl, combine the coconut oil, coconut butter and the pumpkin puree and stir until well combined.

Add erythritol or any other keto friendly sweetener of your choice and the pumpkin pie spice. Cinnamon will do just fine if you don't have the pumpkin pie spice.

87

Once the batter is well combined, pour it into an ice cube tray or candy molds.

Lastly, place some chopped pecans on a dry pan and toast them up over medium heat until fragrant and slightly browned. This step is completely up to you but toasting the pecans brings out a nuttier flavor.

Gently press some pecan pieces on the top of each fat bomb so that they adhere.

Refrigerate until set.

Enjoy!

Nutritional info per serving: Calories 125, Proteins 1g, Carbs 1g and Fats 1g

Easy Lemon Fat Bombs

Prep time: 5 minutes

Cook time: 0 minutes

Inactive: 30-60 minutes

Total time: 35 to 65 minutes

Yields: 10 fat bombs

Ingredients

15-20 drops of stevia extract (lemon or clear)

1-2 teaspoons of lemon extract or 1-2 tablespoons of organic lemon zest

¼ cup (2 oz. / 55g) extra virgin coconut oil

7.1 oz. /200g of softened coconut butter

Optional:

Pinch of pink Himalayan salt or sea salt

Directions

Zest the lemons then ensure that the coconut oil and coconut butter are softened (at room temp). To avoid having large pieces of the lemon peels in your fat bombs, it is better to use a very fine grater.

Place all ingredients in a bowl and mix ensuring that the stevia and lemon zest are evenly distributed – if you prefer a less bitter (maybe caused by too much stevia) and sweeter taste, use powdered erythritol instead or 2-4 tablespoons.

Spoon a tablespoon of the coconut mixture into silicon candy mold or mini muffin paper cups then place on a tray.

Place the tray in the fridge until the fat bombs solidify – takes 30-60 minutes.

Keep the fat bombs refrigerated a coconut butter and coconut oil get soft at room temperature.

Enjoy!

Nutritional info per serving: Calories 112, Proteins 0.76g, Carbs 2.9g and Fats 11.9g

Peaches And Cream Fat Bombs

Prep time: 10 minutes

Cook time: 0 minutes

Freeze time: 4 hours

Total time: 4 hours 10 minutes

Yields: 24 servings

Ingredients

3 ½ tablespoons of monk fruit sweetener

¾ scoop of perfect keto peaches and cream ketone supplement

1 cup of frozen peaches, warmed slightly

6 oz. softened cream cheese

4 tablespoons of unsalted Kerrygold butter, softened

Directions

Using a hand mixer, mix together the peaches and cream ketone supplement, peaches, cream cheese, 3 tablespoons of monk fruit sweetener and butter in a medium sized bowl until well combined.

Scoop the mixture into silicon molds then top each with the remaining monk fruit sweetener.

Freeze the molds for 4 hours on the freezer.

Remove the fat bombs from molds once frozen and enjoy.

Nutritional info per serving: Calories 43, Proteins 0.5g, Carbs 1g and Fats 4.2g

Cinnamon-Roll In A Mug

Prep time: 2 minutes

Cook time: 1 minute

Total time: 3 minutes

Yields: 1 serving

Ingredients

For the Cinnamon Roll

1 egg

2 tablespoon of melted butter

1 tablespoon of Lakanto classic

1 teaspoon of cinnamon (less if desired)

½ teaspoon of baking powder

3 tablespoon of almond flour

For the Icing:

½ T Lakanto Confectioner's

1 oz. Full-fat cream cheese

For the Butter Glaze:

½ T Lakanto Confectioner's

½ teaspoon of cinnamon

1 tablespoon of butter, melted

Directions

In a small Pyrex dish or a large mug, melt 2 tablespoons of butter then add in the egg, truvia, cinnamon, baking powder and almond flour. Mix well until combined.

Place in the microwave and cook on high for 90 seconds. The cinnamon roll will puff up in the mug or Pyrex dish but it won't spill over.

Loosen the cinnamon roll from the bottom of the mug using a fork once the microwave beeps then place on a plate.

For the butter glaze, melt the butter then add in the truvia and cinnamon and mix well. For added moisture, texture and sweetness, pour the butter glaze over the cinnamon roll.

Microwave the cream cheese in the Pyrex bowl or mug on half power until the cream cheese starts to crackle for around 30 seconds. Add in ½ a tablespoon of the truvia and mix well. Pour this cream cheese "icing" on top of the copycat cinnabon and enjoy while warm.

Nutritional info per serving: Calories 599, Proteins 14.4g, Carbs 6g and fats 57.2g

Strawberry Cheesecake Fat Bombs

Prep time: 15 minutes

Cook time: 0 minutes

Total time: 2-3 hours

Yields: 12 servings

Ingredients

½-1 tablespoon of vanilla extract or 1 vanilla bean

2 tablespoons/20g powdered erythritol or 10-15 drops of stevia

¼ cup/ 60g coconut oil or butter, softened

150g/ ¾ cup of cream cheese, softened

½ cup/ 70g of strawberries, frozen or fresh

Directions

In a mixing bowl, place the butter (or coconut oil) and cream cheese cut into small pieces then leave at room temp until softened for 30 to 60 minutes.

Ensure that the butter is softened; otherwise, it will be difficult to achieve a smooth texture and to mix - Don't microwave the butter as the mix needs to stay firm.

Meanwhile, wash the strawberries thoroughly and remove the green parts. Place the strawberries in a blender and blend for smooth texture or place in a bowl and mash with a fork.

Add the vanilla extract or vanilla bean and the powdered erythritol or stevia and mix well. Ensure the strawberries have reached room temp before mixing them with the rest of the ingredients.

Add this mixture to the bowl with the softened cream cheese and butter then mix using a food processor or a hand whisk until well combined.

Spoon the mixture into candy molds or small muffin silicon molds then place in the freezer until set for about 2 hours.

Unmold the fat bombs when done setting then place into a container. Keep in the freezer while you enjoy one at a time.

Nutritional info per serving: Calories 67, Proteins 0.96g, Carbs 0.99g and Fats 7.4g

Jalapeno Poppers Fat Bombs

Prep time: 10 minutes

Cook time: 30 minutes

Total time: 40 minutes

Yields: 6 servings

Ingredients

1 oz. /29g/2 jalapeno peppers, seeded, halved and chopped finely

¼ cup/30g of grated cheese or Gruyere cheese

4 slices/120g of no sugar bacon

¼ cup/55g ghee or unsalted butter at room temp

3.5 ounces/ 100g full fat cream cheese at room temp

Directions

Process the butter (or ghee) and cream cheese in a food processor or mash together in a bowl until smooth.

Preheat your oven to 160 degrees C or 325 degrees F (or gas mark 3).

Use parchment paper to line a rimmed baking sheet. Ensure that you use a rimmed baking sheet to contain bacon fat as it is required in the recipe too.

Lay the bacon slices onto the prepared baking sheet ensuring you leave enough room between them so they don't overlap.

Place the baking sheet into the preheated oven and cook until crispy for 25 to 30 minutes. The thickness of the bacon slices determines the exact amount of cooking time.

Remove bacon from the oven and leave to cool. Crumble the bacon in a bowl once cool enough to handle and set aside

To the butter and cream cheese mixture add the bacon grease, jalapenos and cheddar cheese (or Gruyere cheese) then mix well to combine.

Refrigerate until set for 30 minutes to 1 hour. Divide the mixture into 6 pieces then place on a parchment lined plate. Roll them in the crumbled bacon if serving immediately until well coated. Refrigerate without the bacon if serving later in an airtight container for up to a week – once ready to eat, roll the fat bombs in reheated or freshly cooked bacon crumbs before serving.

Nutritional info per serving: Calories 208, Proteins 4g, Carbs 2g and Fats 20g

Maple Almond Fudge Fat Bomb

Prep time: 5 minutes

Cook time: 0 minutes

Total time: 5 minutes

Yields: 24 bite sized pieces

Ingredients

1 tablespoon of coconut oil

¼ cup of butter

1 tablespoon of sugar-free zero carb maple syrup

½ cup of all natural almond butter

Directions

Melt the coconut oil, butter and almond butter in the microwave until fully melted together and smooth for 2 minutes stirring every 30 seconds.

Whisk in the maple syrup and stir until well combined.

Set bite sized paper liners inside a mini muffin tin then pour in the mixture and freeze or refrigerate until set for a soft consistency, store them at room temperature and for a firm consistency store in the fridge or freezer

Nutritional info per serving: Calories 60, Proteins 1g, Carbs 1g and Fats 5g

Matcha And Coconut Fat Bombs

Prep time: 7 minutes

Cook time: 0 minutes

Total time: 7 minutes

Yields: 32 fat bombs

Ingredients

For the "truffles"

1 teaspoon of pure vanilla extract

¼ teaspoon of Himalayan salt

¼ teaspoon of ground Ceylon cinnamon

½ teaspoon of Matcha green tea powder

½ cup of full fat coconut milk, refrigerated overnight

1 cup of creamy coconut butter

1 cup firm coconut oil

For the coating:

1 tablespoon of matcha green powder

1 cup of unsweetened coconut, finely shredded

Directions

To a good sized mixing bowl, add all the "truffles" ingredients. Use the hand mixer to mix together the ingredients on high until fluffy and light then place in the refrigerator for about an hour to firm up.

Meanwhile, in a fairly large mixing bowl, combine the matcha powder and the shredded coconut together then set aside.

Form the firm truffle mixture into 32 bite sized balls using a small ice cream scoop – roughly the size of a ping pong ball.

Place the balls between your palms and roll them into perfect spheres then roll the balls into the matcha/coconut mixture until completely coated.

Place the fat bombs in an airtight container and store in the refrigerator for up to 2 weeks.

You can eat the fat bombs straight out of the refrigerator or allow them to sit at room temp for 10 – 15 minutes before eating them.

Nutritional info per serving: Calories 135, Proteins 0.8g, Carbs 2.9g and Fats 13.9g

Waldorf Salad Fat Bombs

Prep time: 5 minutes

Cook time: 0 minutes

Total time: 25 to 35 minutes

Chill time: 20 to 30 minutes

Yields: 6 servings

Ingredients

2 cups/70g of pecans or walnut, roughly chopped

2 tablespoons/5g of chopped spring or fresh chives

¼ teaspoon of onion powder

¼ teaspoon of garlic powder

½ small (60g) green apple, diced into half-inch pieces

½ cup (65g) crumbled blue cheese

2 tablespoons (28g) ghee or unsalted butter at room temp

3 ounces (85g) of full fat cream cheese at room temp

Salt and pepper to taste

Directions

Process the butter or ghee and cream cheese in a food processor or mash together in a bowl until smooth.

Add the chives, onion powder, garlic powder, apple and the crumbled blue cheese then stir to combine. Season with pepper and salt.

Refrigerate until set for 20 to 30 minutes.

Use an ice cream scoop or a large spoon to divide the mixture into 6 balls then roll the balls in the walnuts or pecans.

Enjoy immediately or place in an airtight container and store in the refrigerator for up to 1 week.

Nutritional info per serving: Calories 193, Proteins 4.5g, Carbs 4g and Fats 19.3g

Red Velvet Fat Bombs

Prep time: 15 minutes

Cook time: 40 minutes

Total time: 55 minutes

Yields: 24

Ingredients

1/3 cup of heavy cream, whipped

1 teaspoon of vanilla extract

3 tablespoons of natvia

100g of softened butter

125g of softened cream cheese

100g of 90% dark chocolate

4 drops of keto friendly red food coloring

Directions

In a heatproof bowl, melt the chocolate over a small pot of simmering water. Ensure that the bowl is not touching the water; otherwise, the chocolate will burn.

Use a hand mixer on high speed to mix together the remaining ingredients while the chocolate is melting until fully combined for 3 minutes.

Slowly pour the chocolate mixture to the other ingredients with the hand mixer on low speed then mix for 2 minutes on medium speed.

Add the mix to a piping bag then pipe it onto a lined tray. Place in the fridge for 40 minutes.

Place the heavy cream in a whipping canister then apply the whipped cream to the fat bombs.

Nutritional info per serving: Calories 59, Proteins 0g, Carbs 0g and Fats 6g

Dark Chocolate Coffee Fat Bomb

Prep time: 0 minutes

Cook time: 5 minutes

Freeze time: 20 to 30 minutes

Total time: 25 to 35 minutes

Yields: 4 servings

Ingredients

8 oz. of coffee

2 tablespoon of dark cocoa powder

6 tablespoon of butter

4 tablespoon of coconut oil

Directions

Place the butter and the coconut oil in a bowl and melt in the microwave.

Add in the cocoa powder and mix until well combined.

Distribute the mixture evenly among 4 silicone baking cups – about 4 tablespoons per cup) then place in the freezer for 20 to 30 minutes.

Next, put 1 fat bomb to a coffee mug then brew coffee over it before adding in stevia and heavy cream as desired for taste.

Mix well and enjoy.

Nutritional info per serving: Calories 275, Proteins 0g, Carbs 2g and Fats 31g

Baked Pecan and Brie Prosciutto Savory Fat Bomb

Prep time: 2 minutes

Cook time: 12 minutes

Total time: 14 minutes

Yields: 1 serving

Ingredients

1/3 teaspoon of black pepper

6 pecan halves, (1/3 ounce)

1 ounce of full at brie cheese

1 slice of prosciutto (1/2 ounce)

Directions

Preheat your over to 375 degrees F.

Use a muffin tin with muffin holes that are about 1.5" deep and 2.5" wide.

Fold the prosciutto slice in half so that it looks almost square then place it in one muffin hole to line it completely.

Chop the brie cheese into cubes and leave the white skin on then place it in the muffin hole lined with the prosciutto.

Place the pecan halves amongst the brie then bake until the prosciutto is cooked and the brie is melted for about 12 minutes,

Allow to sit for 10 minutes before removing the fat bombs from the muffin pan.

Nutritional info per serving: Calories 183, Proteins 1g, Carbs 0.43g and Fats 16g

Savory Mediterranean Fat Bombs

Prep time: 10 minutes

Cook time: 35 minutes

Total time: 45 minutes

Yields: 5 servings

Ingredients

5 tablespoons (25 g / 0.9 oz.) of parmesan cheese, grated

2 cloves of garlic, crushed

4 olives (12 g / 0.4 oz.), pitted (kalamata or any other type)

4 pieces (12 g / 0.4 oz.) of Sun-dried tomatoes, drained

2-3 tablespoons of freshly chopped herbs (oregano, thyme and basil) or 2 teaspoons of dried herbs

¼ cup (55 g / 2 oz.) of butter or ghee, softened at room temp

½ cup (100 g / 3.5 oz.) of cream cheese, full-fat

1/4 teaspoon of salt or more to taste

Freshly ground black pepper

Directions

Cut the butter into small pieces then place in a bowl with the cream cheese. Place in the kitchen counter and leave it for 20 to 30 minutes to soften.

Mash using a fork then mix well until combined. Add the chopped kalamata olives and the sun-dried tomatoes.

Add in the crushed garlic, dried herbs (or freshly chopped) and season with pepper and salt.

Mix well then place in the refrigerator to solidify for 20 to 30 minutes.

Remove from the fridge then shape them into 5 balls – use an ice cream scooper or a spoon.

Roll each ball into parmesan cheese (grated) then place on a plate.

Eat immediately or store in an airtight container in the fridge for up to a week.

Nutritional info per serving: Calories 164, Proteins 3.7g, Carbs 2g and Fats 17.1g

Conclusion

We have come to the end of the book. Thank you for reading and congratulations for reading until the end.

If you found the book valuable, can you recommend it to others? One way to do that is to post a review on Amazon.

Don't forget to leave a review for this book on Amazon!

Do You Like My Book & Approach To Publishing?

If you like my writing and style and would love the ease of learning literally everything you can get your hands on from Fantonpublishers.com, I'd really need you to do me either of the following favors.

1: First, I'd Love It If You Leave a Review of This Book on Amazon.

2: Check Out My Other Keto Diet Books

KETOGENIC DIET: Keto Diet Made Easy: Beginners Guide on How to Burn Fat Fast With the Keto Diet (Including 100+ Recipes That You Can Prepare Within 20 Minutes)- New Edition

KETOGENIC DIET: Ketogenic Diet Recipes That You Can Prepare Using 7 Ingredients and Less in Less Than 30 Minutes

Ketogenic Diet: With A Sustainable Twist: Lose Weight Rapidly With Ketogenic Diet Recipes You Can Make Within 25 Minutes

Ketogenic Diet: Keto Diet Breakfast Recipes

Fat Bombs: Keto Fat Bombs: 50+ Savory and Sweet Ketogenic Diet Fat Bombs That You MUST Prepare Before Any Other!

Snacks: Keto Diet Snacks: 50+ Savory and Sweet Ketogenic Diet Snacks That You MUST Prepare Before Any Other!

Desserts: Keto Diet Desserts: 50+ Savory and Sweet Ketogenic Diet Desserts That You MUST Prepare Before Any Other!

Ketogenic Diet: Ketogenic Diet Lunch and Dinner Recipes

Ketogenic Diet: Keto Diet Cookbook For Vegetarians

Ketogenic Diet: Ketogenic Slow Cooker Cookbook: Keto Slow Cooker Recipes That You Can Prepare Using 7 Ingredients Or Less

Note: This list may not represent all my Keto diet books. You can check the full list by visiting my Author Central: amazon.com/author/fantonpublishers or my website http://www.fantonpublishers.com

Get updates when we publish any book on the Ketogenic diet: http://bit.ly/2fantonpubketo

Closely related to the keto diet is intermittent fasting. I also publish books on Intermittent Fasting.

One of the books is shown below:

Intermittent Fasting: A Complete Beginners Guide to Intermittent Fasting For Weight Loss, Increased Energy, and A Healthy Life

Get updates when we publish any book on intermittent fasting: http://bit.ly/2fantonbooksIF

To get a list of all my other books, please visit fantonpublishers.com, my author central or let me send you the list by requesting them below: http://bit.ly/2fantonpubnewbooks

3: Let's Get In Touch

Antony

Website: http://www.fantonpublishers.com/

Email: Support@fantonpublishers.com

Twitter: https://twitter.com/FantonPublisher

Facebook Page: https://www.facebook.com/Fantonpublisher/

My Ketogenic Diet Books Page: https://www.facebook.com/pg/Fast-Keto-Meals-336338180266944

Private Facebook Group For Readers: https://www.facebook.com/groups/FantonPublishers/

Pinterest: https://www.pinterest.com/fantonpublisher/

4: Grab Some Freebies On Your Way Out; Giving Is Receiving, Right?

I gave you 2 freebies at the start of the book, one on general life transformation and one about the Ketogenic diet. Grab them here if you didn't grab them earlier.

Ketogenic Diet Freebie: http://bit.ly/2fantonpubketo

5 Pillar Life Transformation Checklist: http://bit.ly/2fantonfreebie

5: Suggest Topics That You'd Love Me To Cover To Increase Your Knowledge Bank. I am looking forward to seeing your suggestions and insights; you could even suggest improvements to this book. Simply send me a message on Support@fantonpublishers.com.

PSS: Let Me Also Help You Save Some Money!

If you are a heavy reader, have you considered subscribing to Kindle Unlimited? You can read this and millions of other books for just $9.99 a month)! You can check it out by searching for Kindle Unlimited on Amazon!

Made in the USA
Middletown, DE
26 June 2019